DISTANCE

ROSE

First Published in 2020

Becomeshakespeare.com

One Point Six Technologies Pvt Ltd.
119-123, 1st Floor, Building J2, B - Wing,
Wadala Truck Terminal, Wadala East,
Mumbai, Maharashtra, India, 400022.
T:+91 8587995915

Wordit Art Fund helps deserving authors publish their work by providing monetary support. To apply for funding, please visit us at www.BecomeShakespeare.com

Copyright © 2020, Rose

Illustrations - Shilpa Bharti

All rights reserved. Any unauthorized reprint or use of this material is prohibited. No part of this book may be reproduced or transmitted in any form or
by any means, electronic or mechanical, including photocopying, recording, or by any information storage and retrieval system without express written permission from the author/publisher.

Please do not participate in or encourage piracy of copyrighted materials in violation of the author's rights. Purchase only authorized editions.

©

ISBN - 978-81-947726-5-1

DEDICATION

For readers.

ACKNOWLEDGEMENT

The stages of distance book publication were funded by Word Art Fund. I am hugely grateful for their initiative that helps budding authors publish their work.

Notes

Aphrodite's myrtles- myrtles is sacred to the mythological Greek goddess Aphrodite.

Apollo holes/ Venus holes- Two tiny ditch like structure over back on the waist.

Karta- close one to the dead person who gives fire to the pyre.

Mahua- Madhuca longifolia is an Indian tropical tree.

Contents

Contents

FALL

Go on, grab the seat;

peel oranges; its flare;

break lettuce; the knife run over bread;

cheese sponge fumbles between teeth;

notice its flavor stumming throat

and thump your palm on the table with frustration.

Like an egg your brain cuts into halves,

 bones strew inside broth;

You can taste your flesh and sweat

and deny your inner core over

Blatant bellow—

"You see yourself through him"

DEWDROPS

When Spirea lades its bottom on a stem; bees
pierced my solitude;

Along buzz comes the note unfurling its leafless
bloom,

Tempest lurk in my nook, it was unexpected

Or an expected desire—a friend's birthday invitation
from her friends,

To please the summer and my empty brook, I dressed
and

Fall at her door;

To watch her is like watching an ivy strum along
birds hum and

Sparrow chirp;

Announced by the bell of nights, arrives the silence;

I took a walk beside the ivy and listen to her words—
cascade—the fall,

Cut through my lands in streams.

Summer tint–

Two buds proclaim

spring.

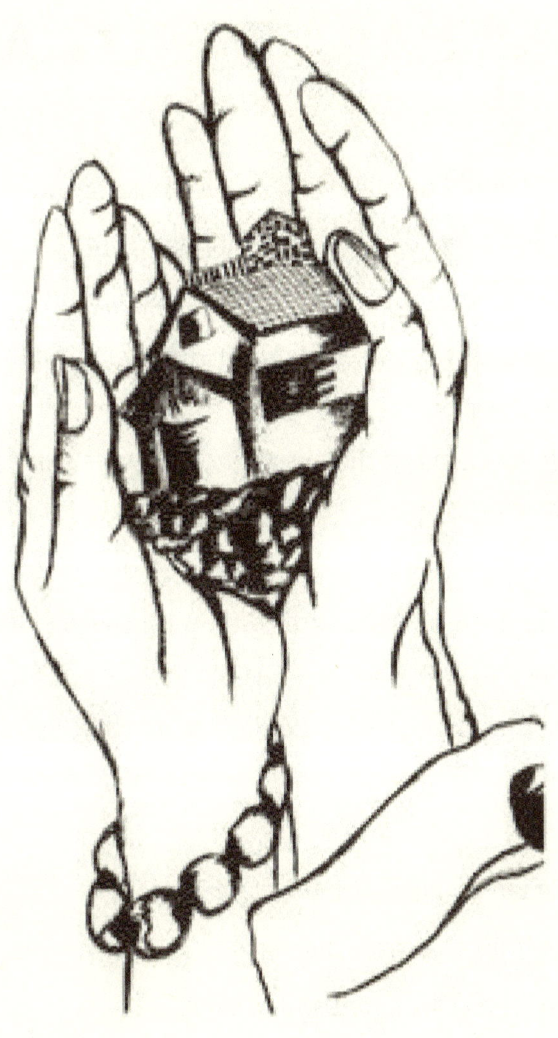

MI CASA ES SU CASA

He couldn't remember;

What propelled him to take these stairs?

(Minor entanglement or sweet rendezvous);

Towards the street besides running traffic to
fragments;

He sits around the river and judges its bend in
disarray;

The flock of Ibises litter dusk with soggy clouds
weight on wings,

Behind that gathered buildings sun settles over the
city;

He would glare it with popped eyes;

As if for the first time,

for him—Clock had sailed slow;

The man, who is in love slough their days,

Washing, polishing themselves;

Before spring he bends knees; collect the ample

to hold and encapsulate it; against all odds;

So when She—"what is the type of our relation _ _
_"

Right there he shunts her lashes with hands and

whisper " **my home is your home**"

SCOUT'S ISLAND

The scout discovered her, god strain rays, only the chosen one shine upon her face shares shimmer with airy goods. Warm feelings replaced excitement, halo mound his hair, he became an angel who looks after her.

She: his fantasy island—more than her, his vein explores--

dizzying highs-

exquisite middle-

creamy lows-

BRAE CURVE

He is accustomed to climbing heights.

Night is burning black paper, time stops when
she toss-roll, feathery fingers cringe his shirt. Her
curves mighty mountains brae—one human habitat
at the brow—spotless beauty spot on waistline. He
walks till there; lips peck the door. Fantasy awaits
him. The divide springs stream fills his steaming
bowl till the brim. Aphrodite's myrtles embellish
the col. The ridges throw question on him; one tiny
stone from the cairn asks about his love for her,
second stone narrates lengthy stories. She leans her
head; his beating chest states.

Fat Sky lower its weight, clouds like stuffed toys
pouch moisture swings on the mountain's cap, she
sucks their freezing water, his arms-fitting jacket
hold her frozen body tight as seat belt of cars do in a
crisis, passionate match lit her warm, white colour
overlaps blue uncover yellow, To-Fro moving flames
goes scarlet red, it burns her like a candle, she melts
on his palm flee through his fingers as slipping sand
inside an hourglass, time slide in their lenses.

BLUEBELLVINE

Bequeathed fingers; straps nape–digging deeper in hair; clinch, plucking tendril strands, pulling closer and closer.

Her face almost abuts Philtrum. Then, starving lips Feast–speck, sips contours on her mouth.

Hankering palm lines decipher riddle–treasure trove heaven bestowal–two bosoms.

Paradise blow astounds breathe; pith black hair sigh cascade dandelions into the lake–Venus holes and navel–tender cherries sapor.

His tongue sprint lateral undulation draws pattern. Bluebellvine petal folds and ridge open chasm emanate milk and honey, His supper between her thighs.

MORNING PLAY

After night shut in cheery sweat,

Grapes; wetness on the roof;

let me not talk of coffee beans

which might fuel this process;

to wake you from morning sleep

is like crossing countries.

I trace your curves, to check staccato;

Minim, crotchet; sparks found these nodes;

I board the trails of your anterior front;

This tongue bought to you the mouthful of the sea;

The breakfast table is left in mess;

crumbs from floor to floor;

you push me

onto the same tabletop

and eat from my divinity.

HIDDEN BAILIWICK

What it is to unveil from drapes

And was your skin a wax-satin with the tallow of
lavender oil;

Igniting flares in mine; the fire lurks in this room or
us?

You are burning batch and cullet baked hot;

Molding into something—

which could fit me;

My hands are the hands of forger;

fingers mending ways to hold, to cradle

 amber glow of your bright fields and brazen out the
sound inbreathes,

until the sun soften into

my bare hands.

love is peacock's wing

it comes

in hues of color

US OR NOT

The young women sit in our garden;

Holding all the dried leaves of fall;

She is not cleaner, I insist;

Which cleaner wear such a pair of shoes while cleaning?

Beside her—there is a man;

Not exactly the man but the thick shadow of him

 tossing her life ;

her eyes blaze Desolation, despair, dreads of betrayal;

places: I never wish to pay a visit too;

from our room; We saw her,

my fears— the future of us collided with her fate and

 Kept sealed in my mouth.

LUMINOUS

Abandon luminous love—thrown onto the attic, is forgotten.

Now; decorated by granules of dust—

deary rust to get rotten.

We outgrow love!

let it suffocate until it recurs in fashion again.

RIDE ALONG

Ride along with happiness, he surpasses in the flash of a second!

Walk with sadness, his sluggish troll, ho-hum swing in time,

He becomes a good companion...

"Gloomy days,

will this storms boom"

WOMB

It was some time ago, with care two firm hands dig;
plough her stomach, just beneath her navel a seed
pour; Nine-month nurturing process. Hairy clouds
afloat, ephemeral bark abrasive texture wear finger
ring; the moon and the sun becomes eyes without
lashes, blood fades its colour while skin drifts in
transparent water; birds begun to dive in face,
bosoms two mountain heaps, frozen skin glacier
sail boats on seas, shooting stars duck through the
throat, the Apollo holes hides lost Atlantic city, wild
lives inside raised arced underfoot—

inside womb;

when she carry a child;

the women becomes the earth.

GLASS, PAIN

Panes of glass cover his mind

but not separating her from the scenery......

Someday he might act...

She will crumble in space bought by him...

IMMORTAL COLOSSAL

Autumn night–

On my pillow

The crows

Feather.

"THIS STORY WAS WRITTEN WITH BLACK FEATHERS"

I

Nobody would give rest to such morning in their lives;

I cannot occupy myself into the crooks of

 this cloud: tangerine, cadmium yellow ;

it is sleek in speaking of tales in monochrome.

Somebody slit all the robins head; preen these pots of peonies for

Delphinium to grow soon out of it;

If anyone could bring me the casket;

I would look into the wide spaces and find myself

Unable to put something—too small that died in my womb out into the box.

II

Many days,

before this unfaithful morning,

he bent himself Into the maze

— the puzzle impossible

for me to solve.

PISTIL OVER EAR

Dandelions seed balls—my vulnerability is lustrous protruding white hairy flocks on a Capitulum.

Speaking to someone is like going through throat tunnel of an excavated faces; through their mouths, I walk splashing on voices puddle, splattered words bathe my jeans up to knees; my braids loosen hair;

Shrugging folds of my leather jacket rubs against tension;

How? Scary is to sense, one hefty breathe, one blow from the end turns my furs to less revealed destination—An Attempts of recollecting each one is the failure that startles on my face. I will lose to their power and become—the heap of flesh levitating like pistil in hands of kids, on people's skin or dog's ear.

GRIEF TO ME

She—"grief looks to me-permanent room-mate,

It loves me with its blood, I cannot push it out.

It is stale food that I mistakenly eat, my oral embouchement throws back-spoiled pudding as drunken human puked rotten cake, and the lamps shining on streets above white-yellow thermoplastic marking cannot be my hope.

It is a punishment given to a soldier for not being trained to live in the world, poles of hand-holding gun running across stadium forever.

It is a misbehaving hound in my neighborhood; my meatloaf fills its grotesque.

It is one of those creatures, you might find in Horror thrillers, a phantom,

It stuffs cotton in my mouth and threats me on my trial to leave."

BACKYARD MIND

When I see the cupboard at the corner of this room;

Its brass knob and jammed keyholes guarding things

Form anyone's sight; it reminds me of my body
trying to

Hold days tight into the skin: warm,

It's potential to burn me alive, the whispering dry
winds

and long-gone days.

The night remains as it is; my stomach splits into
melons,

mind match to fall;

In the line of memorized memory; can I go gentle
into sleep? To escape my radiance where– I suspend
like hinged lilac–nether completely attached, nor
finished on the grounds.

SANDHILL COLT

Her life below grass-top; unstable kite guided by an
immature and like the Sandhill colt,

It drives high, watching man kind's weary bushes.

Her—impetuous courage; scarce wisdom and
credulous innocence afflict by the dart, then the fall
in gold—love.

At the end of meadows and mellows, somewhere
laburnums silence prey upon voices;

It feels safe—walking yards until she drinks it like
the ditch.

LAMENT

I have been travelling in foreign lands,

These new architectural ruins: torn buildings with

*garish crack, Tarnished metal, crippled window
panes;*

beneath my feet this terrace is crumbling sand ;

This city—my inner world: a kingdom through spines

Vanish from bones to bones; blood to blood.

The church has collapsed the bell over its top

*Rumble, after its last gong: The never-ending
silence.*

Winter truth

Stabs doesn't heal for

Forever.

KARTA

What would you buy for the soul who departed?

Off- course, white flower—mourning flora.

*Ashes from the south, air companion vanish, sacred
water's ice-penitent blow freeze it's remnant,
through fires lamps-- water's garland it listens to
bells, conch horns, humming hymn offering to stone.
The stone remained still-deaf, smile reruns its face,
emotions puzzles it, ripe mahua's sweet empathy,
Yew's poison jealousy, palm wine pleasure, grief
barks on ghoul's whistle, sadness munch on people;
maggots on a corpse. In holiness it gazes and smiled
at me, fettering hope that invites ritual supposed to
ease farewell.*

*for a while casket have been my home, marigold
embellish my hair, luxury bath wipes me off, I smell
of sandal in radiant angelic clothing, before entering
its gate, it comforted my spine like cotton candy,
smooth without any mangled mess, the lull of cries
crowds me. I parade across gully, lane beside houses;*

I perform drill with marigold blanket. Orange is my colour for the day, the love wears white. My new jobs joining letter made a shift.

Pyre is my home now: it's hot, my skin lacks water, breaking woods–grinding creature whose furnace never scarce off fuels, so I packed my memories, growling experience and leave...

Love (Karta) encroach white flower seven inches down my throat.

UNIVERSE CONSPIRE

Here I sit on a stool at cafe, where I usually sit; scanning through the menu.

What If, the universe conspire lives? I become a diligent observer.

A woman, dressed in white, clad in my opposite. Slight tilt on her face points straight to her toes, speaks she is lonely.

Loneliness comes in its own size and packaging; few are small gems on her ring dance upon her finger; few are the lengthier chapter that takes decades to read. Some floats across Perennial River clashing rocks, in quiet, lurid weather it cracks the sail and blurb hull against my feet. Waterfall splash, it navigates with disturbing tide crosses, clouds, valleys, canals, fishes puff lungs and burp it at shores. Many have swept by her hands away by an uncanny event,

We lose us in some circumstances; it can be dead or disaster or suppose someone who leave and never return or might fall for another human.

I let myself tear this night so my fall could begin

So I could see myself from distance in the form of the women in white dress;

Until this decay's smell would fade and

I rise again,

I rise again...........................

ABOUT THE AUTHOR

Shilpa Bharti, pen name- Rose, literature lover sketch artist and aspiring author cum poet.

Distance is her debut poetry book. She is Jawaharlal Nehru University, Delhi, India 2019 batch graduate in language and social studies. Anything that makes her lark chirp is reading books and literature work along with sketching and various forms of the related art. Ranchi, Jharkhand is her childhood home town. She had published in several literary journals. She hopes to continue writing as a part of her life. Readers can reach her through—

Instagram-(ruby_rose.writer),

twitter (@RoseChanging),

Youtube (poetic lineage)

www.ingramcontent.com/pod-product-compliance
Lightning Source LLC
LaVergne TN
LVHW041803190726
843493LV00008B/2774